A
Girl's Guide to Being:
A Lady in Waiting
BY
Candice Adewole

This book is dedicated to all the people who inspire me to love and to never give up on my dreams. This book is also dedicated to my future husband; you are worth the wait.

A

Girl's Guide to Being:

A Lady in Waiting

BY

Candice Adewole

Printed in the United States of America

Create Space, 2017

ISBN-13: 978-0692908402

INTRODUCTION

INTRODUCTION

Being a lady in waiting has been one of the most difficult journeys of my life. As a hopeless romantic, all I ever wanted was to fall in love and marry a man who was crazy in love with me too, and create our little family. During high school, I watched on the side lines as my friends were asked out on dates, or to homecoming, or prom. I would often go to the library and get a mountain of teen romance books and sit in my bedroom to read, pining for the day when perhaps one of the guys on the basketball team would ask me out for pizza or to the movies, but it didn't quite happen that way.

Honestly, I found out that being dark-skinned and a little plump was an impediment to my teen dreams coming true, and I was often sought after by guys at my school to be the go between to hook them up with my lighter skinned friends, or skinnier/curvier friends. The rejection hurt. It really hurt, a lot!

It seemed I had finally caught my break when a senior in my health class and I became friends. Initially, I didn't even like him, but we grew on each other, and after a few months of "talking", he asked me to be his girlfriend. I was so happy! I was finally a "normal" teen girl. I had a boyfriend! Of course, my super religious mother was against the entire thing, but gave in when she realized I was not going to let this go without a battle.

Things seemed to be going great for the first few months, but he began to pressure me for sex, using the classic line, "I could be having sex with someone else." With low self-esteem and no masculine protection from a father, I caved and gave in.

I tried to be responsible, so I went to my pediatrician to get birth control – the shot. After seeing a few of my friends and cousins becoming teen mothers, I wanted to make sure I didn't end up another inner-city statistic.

Shortly after, we broke up, so I didn't go back for my next shot. I tried putting the breakup behind me, and decided I would just focus on enjoying the rest of my senior year. Homecoming was nearing and I had arranged to go to the dance with my childhood friend as my escort. Somehow my ex-boyfriend caught word that I was going to homecoming with a date, and the next thing you know he was calling me and we ended up reconciling over Christmas break. Early February, I realized I was pregnant, and if you have read my book *The Black Girl's Guide to Being Blissfully Feminine*, you know how that ended, and it wasn't pretty. What I didn't mention in that book is how when my mother found out I was pregnant, she went down to the Cleveland Clinic and cussed out my pediatrician. Um yeah, the entire experience was a complete nightmare.

My early 20s were scattered with random dates here and there, a few insignificant relationships, and long spells of singleness and celibacy, so I know what being a lady in waiting is all about. The long bouts of singleness gave me time to think, reflect, and grow.

It was after my divorce that I decided to do whatever it took to prepare for the love of my life. This time I would get it right, this time I would be ready to love on the highest level possible. This time the man who I would attract, and be attracted to, would simply be a good guy who wanted to love me.

What would that take? I realized I would need to become a lady in waiting, and I needed to take this time seriously.

This guide is for those women who are waiting for the love of their life to appear. This book will help you get laser focused on the physical, mental, spiritual, and financial changes you need to make to start attracting a different kind of man, and the love you have always dreamed of. My deepest desire is for women to feel good about themselves and to experience the deepest, most intoxicating love ever.

Love,

Candice Adewole

Chapter One: Know What You Want

"It is not a lack of love, but a lack of friendship that
makes unhappy marriages."
— Friedrich Nietzsche

Sitting alone on my bed coming to terms
with the fact that the man I had loved and
prayed so hard for, for 6 years had left me
and was not coming back, I realized that I
could not let this experience break me to the
point where I was unable to love again. I was
going to love again, and I was going to love
even harder than I loved my ex-husband, and
this next man was going to be a great guy
that loved me back the same way. But how
did I get from this sad state to blissful love,
was the pressing question in my heart and
mind? As I began to peel back the layers of

my heart, I discovered there was much work to be done. What about the men in my past had attracted me? Why were they attracted to me? As easy as it is to blame men from our past, we must come to terms with being the common denominators in every single one of our relationships. So, I considered my past and instead of asking what was wrong with them, I decided to ask what was wrong with me.

Soon after separating from my ex-husband, I briefly did some counseling with radio personality, and relationship coach Dedan Tolbert. He is known for his in your face, keep it real advice, something I needed at that moment in my life.

"Candice, your husband never wanted to marry you," he told me bluntly. "This relationship meant absolutely nothing to him, and if you keep allowing him to contact you, and see you, he's going to try using you for sex. You're not emotionally available," he told me.

"But the marriage meant something to me," I said through a very ugly crying fit. Although our marriage really did mean everything to me, because I was IN LOVE with my ex-husband, and the last thing I wanted to do was admit that Dedan was right, I had to explore what he was talking about. Had there been warning signs that I completely ignored? Was I really emotionally unavailable? What did that even mean?

The more layers that I peeled back, the more I realized I *was* emotionally unavailable, and I had been subconsciously choosing to be with men who either didn't want me, or couldn't love me. I was scared to love, and that had to change.

Asking myself the tough questions, meditating, praying, and digging into my feminine essence is what put me in the place I am today. Heart wide open, joyous, and free to love and be loved! It's one of the best feelings ever, and quite honestly, I never thought I'd ever feel like this.

Send me a husband! Dear God, the universe, whoever is listening, SEND ME A HUSBAND!

How many of us have prayed this prayer? My parents were divorced by the time I was seven. My mother, who had been abused by my father, was – from my observation – very leery of men, and as a result, she never dated. I grew up watching my mother live a somewhat anti-social life alone, just her and her bible. I did not want to end up like her. I wanted a husband! I wanted love. I wanted regular, lustful, and passionate sex!

Sadly, I entered the dating world without a clue. I mean, I knew nothing. Nothing of men, marriage, family life, nothing. I didn't know what to look for in a quality man, what quality men were looking for in a wife, or how to tell if a guy was running game. And aside from my uncles who would occasionally stop by to say hello, or show off a new car, I had no men in my life as real examples of what I should be looking for in a man, or how I should expect to be treated.

So, after dating, being married, and then getting divorced, I decided the next time I'd be a bit more specific with my cries to the universe for a man. I'd be intentional and deliberate in my quest for love, because I just didn't have any more time to waste, and I knew at this point that it is simply unwise to go out into the dating world without knowing what you were looking for.

Critical Questions to Ask:

Is the man in question emotionally healthy and ready for a real relationship and marriage? There are many resources and information out there to find the answer to this question, but this is the list I have found effective to weed out the contenders from the pretenders for my precious heart.

1.) Was he raised in a two-parent home, with his dad/stepdad?

If he is from a single parent home, what positive male role models did he have growing up? If he didn't have any positive male role models, grew up on the streets, doesn't know who his father is, or grew up in a house full of women, proceed with EXTREME caution.

Men learn how to be men, and mimic manhood patterns they witness growing up. A lack thereof makes him a questionable partner, as his views on manhood and masculinity may be dysfunctional.

2.) Does he drink excessively or do drugs?

3.) Is he emotionally available?

4.) Can he hold a steady employment/Is he currently employed? If a man does NOT have a job or legal sources of income when you meet him, he is automatically DISQUALIFIED as a potential contender for your heart. Men are the leaders, protectors, and financial providers of the house, and a man without a job cannot provide. Feminine women do not take care of men.

5.) Has he had an excessive amount of sex partners relative to his age? If so, he may not respect women, commitment, or be able to emotionally connect with a woman.

6.) Is he a mama's boy or does he have an unhealthy relationship with his mother? Also look at the relationships he has with the other women in his family.

7.) Is he a work-acholic?

8.) Does he have some sort of spiritual connection? It is important to note that most men are not super religious or spiritual, and need the help of a woman and her femininity to connect deeper to that side of his self.

9.) Does he have any goals for his life? Has he had any major accomplishments in his life if he is at least 30 years old?

10.) If he's over 30, does he still love to party excessively?

These are exploratory questions that absolutely need to be asked. The answers can reveal whether this is a man you want to build a family with. Do not skip, do not pass go, without getting the answers to these questions.

Chapter Two: What Does a Girl *Really* Want?

"Love is patient, love is kind. It does not envy, it does not boast, it is not proud. It is not rude, it is not self-seeking, it is not easily angered, it keeps no record of wrongs. Love does not delight in evil but rejoices with the truth. It always protects, always trusts, always hopes, always perseveres."
— Anonymous, Bible

Over the years, I have gotten a ton of dating advice to just let love come in, don't have any lists, and so forth and so on. However, I believe life gives you contrasts so you can better define your path in life and know what makes you feel good and what doesn't.

Now, without being too picky, I believe you should know what you want in the key areas of a relationship. Those areas are Spiritual, Physical, Sexual, Mental, Social, and Financial.

Take the time to really think about what you want so that you do not settle, and end up regretting the relationship choice you made years down the road. Do this with the understanding that if a man meets the majority of what you want in the key areas, that your love for him can and will grow the more you pour on your feminine nurturing and the more you have frequent sex with him (once engaged or married).

I always advise to have some wiggle room, and be somewhat flexible if you meet a man who is emotionally healthy, shares your core values, and wants to love on you and commit. There is no such thing as a perfect man, so don't turn a good guy down if he hasn't violated your deal breakers list. And you should have a list of deal breakers, the things you absolutely will not tolerate in a relationship.

Chapter Three: Feminine & Fabulous

"Femininity is not just lipstick, stylish hairdos, and trendy clothes. It is the divine adornment of humanity. It finds expression in your qualities of your capacity to love, your spirituality, delicacy, radiance, sensitivity, creativity, charm, graciousness, gentleness, dignity, and quiet strength."

- James E. Faust

One of the most important things you should know as a lady in waiting is that you are powerful simply for being a woman. Not because women are better than men, but because you have been given everything that a man does not have to compliment him (and vice versa), and to bring special feminine gifts to your family, and the rest of the planet.

Men deeply crave our femininity; our soft, delicate, creative, gracious, sensitive, emotional side, because it's everything that is the opposite of him. Our feminine charm is what drive men wild, and becoming increasingly more feminine should be the goal of every marriage minded woman.

Behaving like a man will simply get you treated like a man. Put aside anything you have been taught regarding men and women being equal and know this; You were born equal but different from a man, and we need each other to function wholly.

Fall in love with being a woman and with the special energy you bring. Men are not our enemies, and femininity is our super power, and their kryptonite. A man will lay down his entire life for a feminine woman who captures his heart.

Find ways to increase your goddess power and be magnetic. A few ways that you can be fabulous and feminine everyday:

1.) Be soft. Walk in a manner that is soft and watch your posture. Speak with a soft voice, because women with loud abrasive voices are irritating to say the least. Strive to make your body movements fluid and graceful.

2.) Wear clothing that has soft movable fabric, and in prints, and colors that ooze feminine energy.

3.) Be creative. Dance, sing, write, cook, bake! Do things that evoke feelings of passion. Do anything that gets that creative feminine juice stirred up.

4.) Laugh and be playful. Men are very attracted to women who are in touch with their inner child, provided you don't act like a child when it counts.

5.) Smile and make it your point to change the energy of any room you enter with your feminine presence.

Chapter Four: Date Intentionally

"Being deeply loved by someone gives you strength,
while loving someone deeply gives you courage."
— Lao Tzu

I practiced orthodox Islam for three years
(raised Christian), and the one thing I learned
while practicing Islam is about being
intentional about marriage. In Islam, there is
no casual dating. A man only approaches a
woman with the intent of marrying her. For
most Americans, this is a foreign concept, as
the first question that comes to mind is well
if there is no "dating" then how do they get
to know each other?

In Islam, the etiquette of two singles getting to know each other goes a little like this. A man will approach a woman's father or male guardian (known as a Wali) to make his intentions known for marriage. Then they will strategically get to know each other over a period of about 1-6 months (depending on the culture), and decide to get married by the end of that time frame if things are going well. I actually incorporate a few of these strategies in my Intentional Dating program to help women get to really know a man and get a proposal in the shortest time frame possible.

At any rate, I learned through my experience in practicing Islam that casual dating, seeing what's up, Netflix & Chill dates, looking for friends and free meals, is counterproductive for the marriage minded woman. Going out into the dating world must be for the intent of marriage if that's what you want.

You must make your intent known, NOT in a demanding and forceful way, but by presenting yourself in a manner that says you are the type of woman that any man would want to take home to meet his parents, and saying the right things that will trigger a man to choose you above any of the women he may be currently seeing. Also making it known that you are a traditional woman, with traditional family values, and making sure that your behavior is consistent with that.

A few ways you can be purposeful in your pursuit for love is:

1.) Create a vision board of the kind of man you want. Vision boards can be a powerful manifesting tool, because when you are creating them, and looking at them, it will evoke the energy that helps send signals to the universe that you want that man, and a life with him.

2.) Dress for the role you want. When you are looking to advance in your career, the advice given is to dress like the manager, or those in the position that you'd like to be in. Wanting the position of wife is no different (and is nothing to be ashamed of). Dress in a feminine manner, and be sure to look like the type of woman that a man would marry versus have a short term sexual fling with.

3.) Hang out in places where your ideal man would hang out or go to.

The bottom line is marriage minded women must approach the dating game differently. No longer can you frivolously go on dates, wasting precious time on candidates who are not husband material.

Chapter Five: Prepare for marriage.

"Have enough courage to trust love one more
time and always one more time."
— Maya Angelou

This step is HUGE! In our *Say Yes to the Dress*, blow out wedding obsessed society, people spend more time preparing for the wedding than preparing for actual married life, and we have a divorce rate to prove it. The average couple spends around $27,000 on their wedding, not including the honeymoon, and less than 5% of the wedding budget goes towards premarital counseling or premarital preparedness.

Let's face it: most people in our American culture are more prepared for their chosen career fields than their role as a husband or wife. I truly believe this need to change, because our interpersonal relationships and family bonds are the most important things in our lives, and influence so much of our lives in every area. When you are on your deathbed, I highly doubt you will care or be worried about your career, degrees, or professional advancements. The only thing that will matter will be your family and those you love, so preparing yourself for family excellence and marital bliss is critical.

In *The Black Girl's Guide to Being Blissfully Feminine* I state by the age of 18 our daughters (and sons) should know what to look for in a spouse, as well as have a formal womanhood training on family and home life in addition to seeking education at institutes of higher learning. In tribal societies (and even American culture this training was common place up until the end of the 60's) young girls (and boys) learn the skills necessary to take care of their families and husbands. We need to bring this type training back for the modern woman (and man).

Tips for preparing for marriage:

1.) Read books and listen to videos on marriage. I absolutely LOVE Jimmy and Karen Evans of Marriage Today. They have excellent resources for marriage (Christian based) on MarriageToday.com

2.) Talk to older couples who have a seasoned, yet happy marriage. Wisdom from our elders is priceless.

3.) Find out what heterosexual men actually want and need in a wife. It is a grave mistake for heterosexual women to come up with their own ideas about what heterosexual men need and want from a woman and in a wife. A lady in waiting cannot afford to embrace the negative message of the modern feminist movement that says, "Why should I care what a man thinks or wants?" Unless you plan on sleeping with a vibrator or a house full of cats for the rest of your life, you need to care what emotionally healthy, heterosexual men are looking for in a wife.

4.)   Take marriage preparation courses, including parenting classes. Even if you don't currently have children, you should take parenting classes if you know you want to be a mother one day.

5.)   Learn the feminine arts, and how to care for your home. It is a common mistake, my love, to think your intellect and education alone will help make your marriage and family great. It is equally important to understand how to cultivate a beautiful home life.

Chapter Six: Choose Your Team

"People think a soul mate is your perfect fit, and that's what everyone wants. But a true soul mate is a mirror, the person who shows you everything that is holding you back, the person who brings you to your own attention so you can change your life.

— Elizabeth Gilbert, Eat, Pray, Love

Over the years, American culture has become very focused on the individual. In our culture, we have been taught the key to happiness lies in the pursuit of self, of individual goals and desires, without necessarily giving much thought to what others think or feel regarding the choices one makes.

The truth is many times, and I dare say *most* of the time, the major decisions we make directly or indirectly affect the lives of our families and other loved ones. Because of this I believe the marriage relationship is one area of life we should include our family and trusted friends in, regarding the selection process. Marriage is, after all, about the joining of two families, not just the joining of two individuals.

I know some of you may feel a bit of resistance to the things said in this chapter, because they are against the cultural grain of our society. I implore you, my dear, to keep an open heart and mind.

In one of my favorite Bollywood movies, Kabhi Khusi Kabhie Gham, there is a scene where the son tells his dad that he has fallen in love with this girl and wants to marry her. When his father realizes who it is, he turns to his son and asks him why he thought it was ok to bring that woman into their family. It was a very powerful scene that made me think. Sometimes we are so head over heels in our feelings of love (or lust) for a person that we don't stop to think if the person is truly a good fit for us AND our family. Women who are concerned about creating generational excellence need to care about things like this, not only for the person they choose to bring into their family, but creating standards so that their children and children's children understand they must bring quality people into the family.

1.) Masculine Protection

When dating intentionally for marriage, it is imperative for women to have masculine protection. For most women, the person providing this is going to be their dad.

There is nothing more moving to me than a father being loving and protective over his daughter. Seeing this brings happiness to my heart. Masculine protection is important because men tend to place a higher value and level of treatment on women who have other men in her life that value her highly. It's masculine instinct. You see, when you are dating a man and he doesn't know you from Mary Sue down the street, he starts gathering information about you based on your style of dress, the way you carry yourself, the things you say in conversation, and watching for certain behaviors. Then he starts making assessments AND judgements about your value in his life as a woman and how he should categorize you. However, if you have a man or group of men in your life that place great value on you, and he sees that, he will automatically place a greater value on you and make sure he is treating you the way the man (or men) in your life treat you.

When a guy knows that to get to you he needs to speak to dad, big brother, Uncle Ray, or perhaps all three, he will get his act together, quick! He will be less likely to be disrespectful or pressure you for sex (yes, even grown women). He will instinctively know how to treat you at the same level they treat you.

I advise speaking to your dad ahead of time and letting him know you are intentionally dating for marriage and that you need his help screening men and setting the tone for how you are to be treated. If your dad is already high in his masculinity and protective of you, this conversation may be unnecessary.

I also suggest enlisting the help of your uncles, brothers, grandfather, pastor, imam, or spiritual leader to act as a form of male protection by meeting with the men you are intentionally dating. Also let them know of your desire to marry a good man, and that you will need their help and protection during the intentional dating process, by having them talk to the gentleman or gentlemen in question. I also implore you to be open to their opinions of the man (or men) you may be dating. Men have a way of being able to see through the B.S. of other men.

2.) Wisdom of The Elders

It is always a good idea to seek counsel from those in their golden years, who are loving and wise, and care about you. Their advice is golden!

3.) Keep company with those who love you and support your desire to be married, and be a good nurturing wife. It is essential that you surround yourself with people who actually love and support you, and believe in marriage. You will need this support not only during the courting process, but once you are married to help maintain the marital unit.

Limit time with family members and cut off friends who don't believe in marriage or are always speaking negatively of men. Sometimes many of these people are low key haters and want you to stay single and miserable like them.

I personally have a great team around me. One of them is my personal trainer, Collette Bailey of Yumichic. That woman keeps me right, and gives me constant encouragement and support that my husband is coming.

This year in particular started off really rough as I started having actual panic attacks about the possibility of going through another year single. I had to call on every single person who I knew without a doubt loves me, and ask not for pity, but for their love, prayers, encouragement, support, and positivity, while I wait for my king to come.

The team you have in place is critical to staying protected, loved, supported, and feminine as a lady in waiting. Your team will also allow you to make a more conscious decision on the man you choose to bring into your family and create generational excellence with.

One important note, however. Please make sure the people on your team are emotionally healthy and able to have functional relationships with others.

Chapter Seven: Feel Sexy

"The real lover is the man who can thrill you by
kissing your forehead or smiling into your eyes
or just staring into space."
— Marilyn Monroe

I can tell you from personal experience, that there is nothing like a sex-less and difficult marriage to make you feel horrible and worthless, and to suck all the sexy completely out of your soul. Top that with strict religious dogma, and you have a stale, dry river where feminine juiciness should be flowing throughout your heart and other places south of the border.

My ex-husband and I went seven months without having ANY sex whatsoever, before he finally gained the courage to leave. Prior to this, our sex life was virtually non-existent as we would go several weeks to a month or two without sex for much of the duration of our marriage. It was such an emotionally devastating experience that I honestly didn't know if I could get sexually aroused anymore. Did my lady parts even work still?

I literally had to teach myself how to be and feel sexy all over again. There were some awkward moments, as I struggled for normalcy, and to feel completely comfortable with myself. I had to ask myself when was there a moment in my life where I felt completely happy and sexy? What was I doing at that moment in my life? Once I was able to establish those two things, I rebuilt from there.

Getting your sexy back is important when you are a lady in waiting, not only because it helps you to feel good about yourself and more confident, but it will help you attract men. The energy given off when you feel feminine and sexy is a powerful pheromone; people can't help but feel drawn to you when you are glowing with sexy energy. A few ways you get into the sexy flow:

1.)   Wear red lipstick. There is something about wearing the perfect shade of red lipstick that makes me feel fabulous, and the color red is the color that men are most attracted to. I personally love Ruby Woo from M.A.C. and it looks great on everyone!

2.)   Go salsa dancing. There is something intoxicating about moving your hips to the Congo drums and salsa rhythms, while an attractive gentleman twirls you around on the dance floor.

3.)   Wear dresses that accentuate your feminine curves in a classy way. When you are wearing a well fitted, figure flattering garment, it will naturally boost your confidence and sex appeal.

4.)   Touch on yourself. I'm not talking sacred masturbation here (that's in a later chapter), but what I am saying is take the time to be aware of your body. When you are sitting down I want you to take your fingers and run them up and down your arms, and over your shoulders, and over your legs. Caress yourself. By touching yourself in a loving and sensual way, you can stir up that sexy energy that will help you feel good and be magnetic.

Chapter Eight: Lose Weight

"The best love is the kind that awakens the
soul and makes us reach for more, that plants
a fire in our hearts and brings peace to our
minds. And that's what you've given me.
That's what I'd hoped to give you forever"
— Nicholas Sparks

I touched on this subject in my first book,
from a more cultural point of view, and I still
feel uncomfortable tackling this subject
because of the body shaming campaigns
going strong in this country. I understand
why, as many women suffer from eating
disorders and body image disorders, but as
with many things I believe it has gone far left
field, and there is no balance.

Whenever I address the subject of weight, I always need to make it very clear that women understand I am not saying that women who are overweight don't deserve love, can't get a man, or that a woman's weight is the total sum of her person, or that who she is as an individual soul doesn't matter. I also need to stress that there are a variety of reasons a woman should lose weight and get in shape, and that is namely her health.

However, as ladies in waiting, we need to understand the basic psychology of the heterosexual man. "When we first meet someone, you first notice if you'd like to have sex with them. If you can't see them in that light, there won't be any attraction, and you don't even consider the next levels." (The Science of Attraction, Patrick King).

The truth of the matter, my dear ladies, is this. When a man first meets a woman, the first thing that runs through his mind is does he feel attracted enough to have sex with her. If the answer is yes, then things can progress to the next level of attraction. Aside from wanting to have sex, men will often subconsciously asses a woman's outward appearance to determine if she looks healthy enough to bear children, fit into his social group, and fit his life goals and life pursuits.

So, what does all of this have to do with weight loss? Well, my love, the harsh reality is that most men (on average) prefer women with slender body types, slender curves, fit body types, or what I like to describe as fit/thick body types. Men are visual and their sex drive is aroused and their penises get hard when they see a woman they feel sexually attracted to. A man also wants to remain attracted to the woman he marries, and wants to know she cares enough about herself and her body, not to just let herself go, especially after having children.

It's all about numbers. So, if you are closer to the to the body types that attract the average man (may vary slightly culture to culture), you increase your dating pool numbers. When you are able to increase your dating pool, your odds of finding a suitable partner also increase. I know for some this may feel hurtful, or make you feel sad or uncomfortable, but I relay this message after years of studying male psychology and the science of male attraction.

Modern day feminist rhetoric has made women believe men shouldn't care about a woman's physical appearance and that they should stay focused on the inner being of a woman. That somehow a man wanting his woman to maintain her body shape, or desiring a certain body shape is shallow and sexist, but it isn't. As women, we must understand the basic nature of men, their psychology, and what drives them to do what they do, and think the way they think as men. For men, respect is everything, almost, if not more important than sex! Men are genetically hardwired to compete with other men for food, resources, and women. One of the ways men gain respect within the group of men they associate with is based on the type of woman they choose to be with, so naturally a man will search for the best prize of a woman he can get for himself. This decision includes, but is not limited to, a woman's looks, behavior, intelligence, ability to nurture, special talents, and gifts.

Losing weight during your period of being a lady in waiting is important for a variety of reasons, including your health. Losing weight and getting in shape will also help you feel even better about yourself and more confident.

I recommend consulting with a doctor or weight loss professional before starting a new workout regime. I also recommend enlisting the help of a personal trainer if it is in your budget, or getting a support buddy or group for accountability. If you can't afford a personal trainer, I highly recommend the phone app Aaptiv! It's a cool exercise aap that allows you to access different work outs facilitated by certified personal trainers. Each class is different, and you can select classes based on goals, activities, and fitness levels!

I ask that you take this advice to heart, my dear, and please don't get offended, as this is not my intent. My intent is for you to give yourself an honest evaluation in this area, in order to improve. I want you to be the best version of yourself, and be with the best guy you can possibly be with!

Chapter Nine: Gratitude Journaling

"Once upon a time there was a boy who loved a girl,
and her laughter was a question he wanted to spend his
whole life answering."
— Nicole Krauss, The History of Love

Gratitude journaling is a concept I learned years ago after watching the airing of an episode on the Oprah Winfrey Show, where she spoke about gratitude, and how gratitude journaling had made such an impact on her life. So, I decided I would give it a try, but admittedly it was a short-lived idea.

It wasn't until my nervous breakdown after my divorce that I ran into the concept of gratitude journaling again. I was so desperate to feel happy and a sense of normalcy. I had never in my life felt so depressed, and I needed answers, answers that a life time of praying, fasting, and traditional religion hadn't given me.

I started really studying the laws of attraction, which I knew about, but started studying on a deeper level during this time in my life. The concept of giving thanks, and being grateful kept coming up. It was then that I had made the connection with the power of gratitude journaling and the laws of attraction.

I want to share something extremely powerful with you. Love and gratitude are the two most powerful energetic vibrations on the planet. This may be why every single religion on the plant speaks of love and being thankful.

So, with this knowledge, I revisited the idea of doing daily gratitude journaling. Doing so immediately helped me feel better, and even though some days were repetitive, if I did at least 10-15 mins of pure gratitude journaling, I felt better, and like magic I would find one new reason to be grateful in the moment.

The main reason I want you to get in the daily habit of gratitude journaling is because it will help to keep your spirits positive and focused on the good in your life while you wait for Mr. Right. The other great thing about gratitude journaling is you can give thanks for things that are currently happening in your life, have happened in the past, or things that you want to have happen in the future. The key to writing down the things you _will_ be thankful for, is writing them down in the present tense, example:

I am grateful NOW that my husband is here, or I am grateful that I AM living my dream life.

Doing this gives your gratitude power, and it feels amazingly good. It's very empowering!

Chapter Ten: Erotic Gratitude

"We loved with a love that was more than
love."
— Edgar Allan Poe

If you know anything about me by now, you should know I teach women they should _not_ be having sex as a lady in waiting, and should abstain from sexual intercourse (including oral sex), until you are either married or engaged. The reason for this isn't based on religion, but on male psychology, and the science behind what triggers a man to commit. It is counterproductive for a woman who wants to get married to be having casual sex or having sex with a man she is really into prior to engagement or marriage.

I understand that abstaining from sex can be so difficult for so many, and I can personally understand the struggle as I myself have been celibate now for five years now (since my divorce, longer if you want to count the fact that we weren't having regular sex in the first place.... le sigh). Yes, I said five years! However, if you really want to add Mrs. to the front of your name, and avoid destructive soul ties, you need to keep your legs closed.

One thing I have started doing that has helped to release some of the sexual frustration is to write down erotic gratitudes. These gratitudes are future desires written in the present tense. Writing erotic gratitudes in this way can help you stay in your siren energy, excited about the arrival of your king, and prepare you mentally, and spiritually for having a deeply connected sex life with your future husband, and prepare you for sacred masturbation, a concept I advocate for women to utilize while being celibate. A few examples of erotic gratitudes are:

I am so grateful my husband and I have a very passionate and active sex life.

I am grateful that my husband and I are sexually compatible.

I am grateful that my husband gives me good head.

I am grateful that our love making is lustful and satisfying.

I am grateful that my husband has the perfect size penis for me.

I am grateful that we have a lot of sexual chemistry in our marriage.

You get the idea. Doing this may feel a bit weird and unconventional, especially if you are new to the concept of celibacy, but believe me this does help take the edge off on those days you feel particularly sexually frustrated! It also releases positive sexual energy into the universe.

Chapter Eleven: Meditation & Prayer

"Every heart sings a song, incomplete, until another heart whispers back. Those who wish to sing always find a song. At the touch of a lover, everyone becomes a poet."
— Plato

Meditation and daily prayer is something that has grown into a daily practice for me. Growing up in a strict Christian home, prayer and meditating upon the "word" of God was engrained in me. As I hit my late teens and early twenties, my spiritual life was shaky at best. I would go long periods of time without praying, mostly because I felt guilty for not "living right", and felt unworthy to be heard by God. I struggled with this for years.

My spiritual life strengthened a lot while living in Puerto Rico. Being isolated and living with a very difficult man who was very verbally abusive towards me had taken its toll, and so I turned to my spiritual teachings, because I felt I had nobody else to turn to. My prayer life and reading the bible every day gave me some peace, and led to my conversion to orthodox Islam (which is an entirely different story, and caused further problems in my already very difficult marriage).

After my ex-husband decided to pull another disappearing act after months of dating and trying to "work things out" (we were already divorced, mind you), I fell into a deep depression. I had been depressed before, but not like this. This sort of depression felt as though a piece of my soul was being ripped out and my brain as though it was being rewired (literally, I felt electrical charges wave through my brain, it was a strange experience). I was heartbroken and angry. Angry at God because I didn't understand why, after all the fasting and prayer, he would allow me to go down such a dark spiritual path. I mean, I wasn't asking for much, only love.

I lost all my faith in God, and couldn't even say the word "god" until a few years after, because I felt so abandoned and betrayed by my creator. I experienced hearing voices, and having "things" sit on my bed at night, and crawl on top of me. I cried a lot, and would often sit in the shower naked, balled into a corner pouring my eyes out, trying to figure out why and how all of this was happening to me.

As I struggled to find peace, happiness, and my own identity outside of being someone's wife, I realized I needed spiritual grounding, but not in the traditional sense. I also realized that traditional religious teachings didn't fully give answers to some of what I was experiencing, so I decided that I needed to incorporate some basic spiritual practices that felt good, and would help me get back onto the path of normal. Or the new normal, rather.

For me, the way I pray is different now, as is my definition of prayer. For me, prayer can take many forms, and prayer is the feeling, the thought, the energy, and the vibration you put out into the universe. Prayer can be verbal or non-verbal, and my favorite prayers are those of gratitude and thanksgiving.

These days, my prayers for a husband are silent ones. No more begging or pleading with God/the Universe/Spirit for my husband. I often take the time to give thanks for my husband/lover/best friend/life partner/and soul mate. I send love to him, and connect with his spirit daily, ask for his protection, and ask that he is guided towards me.

During my meditation sessions, I will light candles and focus on love, which is the highest form of energy in the universe. I also focus on my creator, my purpose for being on the planet, my desires, and I always close with gratitudes.

Meditating and praying daily will help keep you grounded and in good spirits during your waiting period. Meditating also helps to activate the laws of attraction which will bring you in alignment with your desires.

Meditation Suggestions:

1.) Music – Meditation music can help keep you focused. I suggest instrumental music that is soft and serene, or sounds of nature. If you choose meditative music that has words, I suggest chant-like songs that have repetitive words like Gayatri Mantra by Deva Premal or Oshun Chant by Women of The Calabash. I personally love those two because of the lyrics!

2.) Light Candles – I absolutely love candles. They add peace and warmth to any environment.

3.) Clean & Quiet Space – You can't very well think straight in a messy environment, so make sure your meditation space is clean and quiet so energy can flow better.

4.) Focus – Focus on what you are feeling. Our feelings have been given to us to navigate our physical existence, and to gauge our point of attraction on the spiritual and physical plane. So, focus on how you are feeling during your prayer and meditation.

5.) Relax, Relate, Release – Utilize your prayer and meditation time to truly let go and relax. Know that all things are working together for your good, and the universe is conspiring to give you what you want!

Chapter Twelve: Sacred Masturbation

"There is nothing in nature like it. Not in robins or bison or in the banging tails of your hunting dogs and not in blossoms or suckling foal. Love is divine only and difficult always. If you think it is easy you are a fool. If you think it is natural you are blind. It is a learned application without reason or motive except that it is God. "

-Toni Morrison, *Paradise*

Whenever anyone mentions masturbation, visions of some old, perverted man, sitting in a dark corner, watching porn, and holding a jar of Vaseline come to mind. Masturbation is rarely talked about as it relates to women doing it, and due to much religious doctrine teaching that one must suppress their sexual desires until marriage (even though there is not one single, solitary scripture that specifically says masturbation is prohibited or a sin), there is much shame and stigma surrounding the practice of masturbation.

What is sacred masturbation? Sacred masturbation is a concept in which you honor the divinity of your sexuality through high vibrational thoughts, energy, and touching of your genitals to bring about sexual pleasure and (but not always) orgasm. The practice of sacred masturbation stems from the "Tantric and Taoist sexual practices which aim to transform raw sexual energy into refined spiritual energy. The Tao Tantric arts, a fusion of these systems offer us feminine practices to guide us to heal, activate, and celebrate our sexual organs, and use our sexual energy as fuel to invite more pleasure, intimacy, energy, health, and joy into all areas of our lives." (www.wildsacredfeminine.com)

For masturbation to be sacred and to have the powerful and beneficial effects on our lives as ladies in waiting, our intentions must be right. "To move from mindless masturbation, to meditative, self-cultivation, we use our intention power, that is our conscious wholehearted attention and awareness. When every single part of us is fully attentive to the sensations of our bodies with a relaxed and loving reverent attitude, then the subtle life of the body has a chance to reveal itself to us, and our sexual experience becomes our meditation and our prayer." (www.wildsacredfeminine.com)

In *The Black Girl's Guide to Being Blissfully Feminine* I touch on the concept of sacred masturbation briefly. I teach this concept as a tool to use to not only get into your sexy, goddess, feminine mode, and stir up positive sexual energy, but I also prescribe it as a means to release sexual energy and stay sexual while abstaining from sexual intercourse during the intentional dating phase.

I have said this more than once, my dears, but it is simply counterproductive to your goal of being a wife to have sex with a man prior to getting the level of commitment you desire, and in our case, that would be engagement or marriage. In these modern times, casual sex and swipe left for hook ups on dating apps like Tinder have become common place. The *Hook Up* culture that has been created as a result has caused so many issues in relationships, women's self-esteem, and women's trust in men.

I speak to many, many women who cannot fathom abstaining from sex for any length of time, let alone waiting until marriage. However, these same women do not understand why they are not getting proposals from men, or are getting used for sex, don't understand why they can't break away from toxic relationships, or have a deep-seated resentment for men in general. I truly believe that sacred masturbation can help with all of that.

Tips for Sacred Masturbation Session:

1.) Focus on the beauty of your female body

2.) Make friends with your yoni – Get to know what your vagina looks like and feels like. Get a handheld mirror and look at your vulva, labia, and clitoris.

3.) Create Ambiance – Utilize candles, music, and scents to create a space that feels pleasurable to all your senses.

4.) Self-massage – Get a massage oil in a scent like sandalwood and find the places on your body that feel good to you.

5.) Use a vibrator, a vibrator is great for clitoral stimulation and achieving orgasm. There are also vibrators on the market that help you to achieve a vaginal G-Spot orgasm, which is even more powerful than a clitoral orgasm! Go between using your fingers and your vibrator to prolong your moment of climax. Take your time!

6.) Enjoy your orgasm – Since there is so much shame surrounding masturbation, focusing on enjoying the overwhelming good feelings that come from having an orgasm is essential. Being open enough to receive the good feelings from having an orgasm is feminine, since being open to receive is a feminine attribute.

7.) Be High Vibrational – Avoid watching porn or having low vibrational thoughts during your sacred masturbation. Remember orgasms are forms of energy, and the energy you give out is the energy you get back!

Chapter Thirteen: Self-Check

"Back then, I confused passions and orgasms with love. It took me years to realize the two weren't synonymous."

-Terry McMillan, *Getting to Happy*

It is absolutely important that you go out into the world of dating with your self-esteem intact. Dating with low self-esteem is a slow death because you will only attract men who further confirm your deepest negative beliefs about yourself and your biggest relationship fears, which will only leave you feeling horrible and with even lower self-esteem than you started with.

I remember struggling with self-esteem for most of my life. I grew up thinking I wasn't good enough, and that I was defective.

When I started dating, I truly didn't believe I was worthy of love, or that I could get the type of man I really wanted. Honestly, I didn't even like myself. I thought I was fat, too dark in complexion, had "bad hair", and was incompetent in so many areas of my life. I didn't even think I was a good mom. I faked perfection because so many people thought I had it all together. I used to hate God for bringing me forth into this physical existence as a Black woman, and I absolutely hated the texture of my hair. Deep down, being me was the last thing I wanted to do or be. I didn't truly believe anyone would want a single, Black woman with a special needs child, but there I was trying to be in a relationship, hoping to find someone to prove me wrong. I was waiting for someone to dig deep down in my garbage bags of brokenness, find "me", then love me.

I thought things would turn out just like one of those sappy, but very romantic Rom-Coms, but sadly it did not. In the movies, the Bridget Jones types often get the guy, fall madly in love, and live happily ever after. In real life, you end up living out a self-fulfilling prophecy, and having your heart broken in pieces.

You can't very well expect someone to love you on a high vibration if you don't even love yourself, let alone *like* yourself. It is unhealthy to think a man can love you, should love you, or would even want to love you, when you don't even care about yourself on that level.

A man instinctively knows when a woman has low-self-esteem, and believe me this is a turn off. There are some men who target women with low-esteem solely to use them for sex. This is a sad, but true fact.

Do you feel worthy of the love you want? This is a very important question to ask yourself, because if you don't believe you are good enough to be loved by a good man, and that man shows up in your life, you won't be able to accept his love.

I remember the few times a really nice guy who genuinely thought I was beautiful and a great woman would come along and try to pursue me and I would feel turned off. Completely turned off. It was only when a man was being difficult, aloof, and mean at times that I would find myself attracted to him, and wanting a relationship from him.

Eventually, I came to realize I was emotionally unavailable and suffering from low-self-esteem, and that is why I found men who had crappy behavior attractive. It wasn't until I really started loving myself, forgiving myself for not being perfect (none of us are anyways), and being emotionally vulnerable, that my taste in men changed, and the type of men I attracted was totally different.

I no longer attract men who try to use me for sex. I only attract men who treat me with respect. I get turned on when men are really nice and I feel 100% worthy of a good man who wants to love me in return! It feels so amazingly good to be in this place.

If you already have a healthy self-esteem, then kudos to you! That is wonderful, but if you have done some self-evaluating after coming this far in the book and realize your self-esteem is not where it should be, I want to leave you a few tips.

1.) Do mirror work- Look at yourself in the mirror and tell yourself daily that you are beautiful, and worthy of love. Say it until you can look yourself in the eyes and believe it.

2.) Explore the reasons why you feel bad. Perhaps you are dealing with residual issues from childhood, or more serious side effects from sexual abuse, substance abuse, or being raised by toxic people.

3.) Seek professional help – I am a huge proponent of going to see mental health professionals, and regularly seek counsel from mental health professionals when I need to. There is absolutely nothing wrong with going to see a counselor or therapist to help you work out your emotional issues. The shameful stigma that comes with seeing mental health professionals needs to end. It is also helpful to see a non-judgmental third party that can help you through your issues and onto a healthier path.

4.) Do daily affirmations – Affirmations are a very powerful tool in helping you change your thought patterns. By verbally affirming positive things about yourself out loud, over time you will begin to believe these things about yourself and deeply internalize them.

5.) Change your associations – As they say, misery loves company, and sometimes to move to a better place vibrationally, you may need to move away from people who are complacent, and love being negative and miserable. Focus on being around people who are genuinely happy in life, because people like this can help raise your spirits which will naturally help you feel better about yourself.

6.) Get dressed up – There is something about taking a nice hot shower, getting dressed up in a pretty dress, throwing on some lipstick, and sliding into a great pair of heels that makes you feel sexy and confident. If you currently don't feel like getting dressed up because you do feel bad about yourself, just fake it until you make it. You WILL get there!

7.) Accept compliments – When someone pays you a compliment, allow yourself to feel good about that, and internalize the positive energy the compliment brings.

Remember, it is critical that you enter the world of dating with good self-esteem. Use this stage in your life to work on feeling good about you, because marriage can, and will, bring out certain issues. You don't want self-esteem issues to be one of them. Trust me!

Chapter Fourteen: Date Yourself

"To return to love, to get the love we always wanted but never had, to have the love we want but are not prepared to give, we seek romantic relationships. We believe these relationships, more than any other, will rescue and redeem us. True love does have the power to redeem but only if we are ready for redemption. Love saves us only if we want to be saved."

- Bell hooks, *All About Love: New Visions*

Aside from going out on actual dates with men, it's important for you to date yourself, and go out on girly dates with friends. Why? Because taking yourself out on dates is a part of loving yourself, and when you are good to you, it shows!

Girly dates with your feminine female friends are important too because female friends are important. They will help you create sisterhood and support. Not only that, having girl time with feminine friends helps keep your femininity on fleek!

One of my favorite things to do is have group "slay" dates, where we go out solely for looking fabulous, laughing, and being seen. For those of you who don't know what the word slay means, it basically means to go out looking fashionable, fabulous, and your absolute best! Friends who slay together, stay together! That's my theory anyways.... lol.

Date Ideas:

1.) Go to the spa: Going to the spa is something you can do by yourself or in a group. Last year, a small group of us went to Jeju Spa, a Korean bathhouse, right outside of Atlanta and it was AMAZING! We literally stayed in the spa for over eight hours and had an absolutely wonderful time bonding.

2.) Go to the movies – I love taking myself to see movies that no one else but me likes. It's nice to just sit comfortably in the theater, and just chill out uninterrupted.

3.) Go out for a nice meal – Treating yourself to a nice meal does wonders to help you feel good about you. The truth is, even though your future husband will be your best friend and you two will have an amazing time doing things together, he may not be available to entertain you 24/7 (he's got to work after all, and even have time with his friends). Learning to entertain yourself will be attractive, because then you won't be a woman who is needy in a bad way that can turn men off.

4.) Have a henna party – I love hosting themed parties. Hire a talented henna tattoo artist in your area, order Indian food, and get a few chick flicks and have some girly fun!

Chapter Fifteen: Say No to Struggle Love

"We love because it's the only true adventure."

- Langston Hughes

Struggle Love. What can I say? This topic can get heated very quickly, especially within the African-American community. The willingness to marry a man who has very little and assist him as he struggles to make it to the top is the heart of what struggle love is all about.

Struggle love also involves choosing to be with a man that makes a certain salary/income and will most likely never make more than that due to his chosen trade or career path, or lack of ambition, and the willingness of a woman to accept this. This is often the place that many women, in particularly African-American women, find themselves, as African-American women often make significantly more than their male counterparts (African-American women currently hold the number one spot for advanced degrees in the United States, regardless of gender or race).

Now, I can't speak for all women, but within the African-American community, we have been engrained from birth to support our African-American men, almost to a fault. We have also been groomed, in most cases, to live life without a man (the irony), or to be willing to settle for a man who may not ever be able to provide us with a comfortable lifestyle.

This grooming seems to be in stark contrast to women of other ethnicities who are told to look for a good man who can take care of them, and be a good financial provider. I could be wrong, but from this side of the looking glass, it seems women of other ethnicities are spared the negativity if they go looking for a man to elevate their current lifestyle.

I do believe the man should be the main provider of the household. This includes, but is not limited to, being the financial provider in the house. My ideologies may seem antiquated, as many modern women don't see any problem with a woman being the primary financial provider in her household, or splitting bills 50/50, 60/40, (or whatever percentage split) with her man, but my beliefs are based on numerous conversations with men, focus groups, and scientific research that has been done regarding the science of attraction, and understanding what creates the balance of masculine and feminine energy as it pertains to relationships.

As a single wife, you need to understand that if you have a man who is masculine at his core (most men on the planet are), he will be driven by his hardwired genetic, masculine, instincts to protect, provide, procreate, and compete with other men for resources, status, food, and women to reproduce his kind and immortalize himself (Way of Men). As a result of these genetically hardwired instincts, most men will naturally feel emasculated when they are with a woman they feel doesn't need him or respect him.

More often than not, a woman making more money and paying all the bills or most of the bills will make him feel emasculated because in his male mind that woman doesn't need him, and sometimes a woman making more money will make him feel further emasculated by bringing up the fact that she makes more money, or not offering enough *"masculine respect"* (yes there is such a thing) simply because she does make more money. This is one reason why some men would prefer to marry a waitress versus a woman with a Ph.D.). Call it fragile male egos if you want to, my dear, but at the end of the day nature wins. There are some things so deeply imbedded within our DNA nothing will change them, even over time.

I think there is nothing wrong with a woman expecting to be provided for, or marrying a man who can provide her with a comfortable lifestyle, or a better lifestyle than she is currently living in. None of these things make a woman a gold digger when she is feminine, intelligent, nurturing, sweet, kind, affectionate, and focused on creating generational excellence.

A few months back, I posted a video on Facebook called "Roommate Mentality Needs to Stop". In this short video, I briefly touched on this topic. The video went viral, and the comments were wild, as you can imagine. Many men were concerned that a woman who expects her man to be the main breadwinner was going to be lazy (sadly mostly African-American men), the second concern brought up in that video was what should be done if the woman makes more money that the man, and my reply was (and always will be) this; if a woman CHOOSES to be with a man who makes less money than her, then she should be willing to live within the means in which he can provide (meaning household necessities), while her portion goes towards other things such as family vacations, college funds, the cable or internet, self-care, gym membership or personal trainer, emergency fund, down payment on a plot of family land, etc., etc.,. If all this man can afford is a two-bedroom condo, and that's who you have chosen to be with, then you need to leave space for him to be feel needed, masculine, and his instincts high, so he will continue to feel the deep-seated desire to protect you and provide for you and your children (if you have any children). Maintaining the energy flow, the yin yang harmony, is very important. When thrown off, it can affect things like sexual attraction. Tantric author David Deida says, "sexual attraction is based on sexual polarity. All natural forces flow between two poles......The masculine and feminine poles between people create a flow of sexual energy in motion." (Secrets of Mind and Reality) (The Play of Sexual Polarity and its effects on relationship choices, www.awaken.com)

This is the honest to God truth, my love. If you know deep down inside that you want to live a certain lifestyle, then don't settle for marrying a man that makes less than what you know would take to maintain that lifestyle. If you get really honest with yourself, you'll realize you will never respect any man you feel you are footing the bill for, or a man who is happy making whatever amount of money he is making and has no plans on changing that.

Now, if you are the type of woman who is willing to be with a man who makes less than you (and it doesn't have to be significantly less), then I've already given you the best advice I can possibly give to maintain yin yang harmony in your home (regarding finances). Personally, I am willing to marry a man who makes less (not significantly less) than me, provided that he is a good man, ambitious, and we are on the same page on the things that really are important regarding life, love, and family matters.

Let's talk a minute about potential. Banking on a man's potential can be risky. We've all heard a horror story or two about some poor woman hanging on to some man's pipe dreams that never came into fruition. Sometimes our nurturing side comes out and we want to be the wind beneath some man's wings, because we can see who he could be if only he tried a little harder.

When it comes to a man's potential there are a few things we must take into consideration, especially my African-American sisters, since we have been culturally engrained to support a man no matter what. If a man truly has potential, and it is worth following his lead in marriage he will:

1.) Be ACTIVELY pursuing his goals. Actions always speak louder than words, because some men can talk a good talk.
2.) Still want to provide for you. A masculine man that is emotionally healthy and high in his masculinity will still do his best to provide for you as much as he can, and with the best he can while he is reaching his goals. Beware of men who want you to foot the bills, and pay for dates in the name of supporting him in realizing his "dreams".
3.) Be making future plans, and strategizing moves for the family to be successful. Men are all about making plans and problem solving, and

executing those plans. If he's not executing the plans he's talking about, he's a pipe dreamer. Leave him in the sewer.

"Women should understand that simply having a plan isn't enough. Goals without plans are simply dreams and if a man has potential to do everything he says he wants to do, but takes no (or very little) actual steps to achieve those goals, it's very unlikely he'll ever get to the finish line………. The thing is, if a man has the potential to do great things and is actively working to achieve those great things, that suggests a much more stable situation. As a woman, if you can see a man with potential doing the necessary work to make himself into whomever it is he wants to be, there's a higher chance he'll be able to fully realize his goals. Potential by itself means nothing, as at some point, one still has to be able to prove they can do whatever they have the potential to do……. Dating a man with potential who is actually doing something to actualize his potential is what makes a man worthwhile……" (madamnoire.com)

This advice regarding potential is mostly for my younger ladies ages 18-26, as the young men you will most likely be dating/courting for marriage will be at the stage of life when they are working towards their goals. If a man is over 30, he should have already accomplished at least one significant goal, and any man in his late 30s, 40s, or beyond should have reached his major goals, or at least have something to show for being on the planet this long.

I don't want women to think they have to settle for struggle love or should settle for struggle love if that's not what they want. I also don't want women to feel guilty for having reached financial success and having money in their bank accounts either. It's ok to want to "marry up", or "marry comfortable", and a woman should definitely be with a man who wants to, and enjoys being a provider. I am personally tired of the cultural expectation for African-American women to be strong, hold down the family, and be _expected_ to help hold things down financially too. As a group of women, we are suffering dearly for this as a result. I could go on and on about this, but I won't.

Could something happen in the unforeseen future to shake things up financially? Yes, something could. Should you stand by your man in an event like this? Of course, but even then, it should be done with the intent of keeping his masculinity high, and maintaining the energy flow, so the relationship doesn't shift, and sexual attraction stays strong. The truth, my dear, is a man will never be the greatest version of himself without a good, feminine woman by his side, and the goal should be to marry a good, emotionally healthy man, who can provide for you not only financially (with household necessities as a minimum), but in other ways too, like helping with the children, house maintenance, etc. It is feminine instinct for a woman to choose the best provider she can for her and her offspring, so don't feel guilty, my loves!

Chapter Sixteen: Money Matters & The Single Woman

I don't know why femininity should be associated with weakness. Women should be free to express who they are without thinking, 'I need to act like a man, or I need to tone it down to be successful.' That's a very good way to keep women down.
- Zooey Deschanel

Money issues account for 40% of all marital problems, and considering how money driven and materialistic our American culture is, you would think we would have all mastered how to manage money as adults, but so many of us haven't. The success of not only your future marriage, but the lineage of excellence you will build with your future husband, depends on how well you can start training yourself to deal with money now as a lady in waiting.

Now as a lady in waiting we should understand by now that we are not paying for dates (except rare occasions and special days like birthdays, holidays, graduations, promotions, etc.), or splitting any bills with men (whether married or not). However, there are many things that you can start to do right now as a single woman to make yourself a powerful asset, and set yourself apart from the rest of the women that are out here.

1.) Start an emergency fund. Having an emergency fund is a good idea anyways, as most people are about 3 paychecks away from homelessness. Having an emergency fund already in place as a lady in waiting can be utilized as a negotiation tool during the engagement phase, and will demonstrate that you are not wasteful of funds and focused on creating generational excellence.

Ellevest is an online investment company that caters to the financial needs of women. Co-founded and run by Sallie Krawcheck, and financially backed by none other than famed tennis player, Venus Williams, *Ellevest* is an excellent tool to use to start an emergency fund and become a bit savvier with the way you save money for generational excellence.

Both my daughter and I have opened accounts with *Ellevest* not only to start saving emergency funds, but for plots of family land, and for our weddings. Feminine power moves like this make you and asset in the eyes of a good masculine man!

2.) Avoid name brands. There is nothing wrong in and of itself with brand names, or even having a taste for the finer things in life, but if everything you buy and wear has a name brand label attached to it, or you feel you must have brand names and nothing else, you are making yourself appear as a financial liability to the average man.

The average man strives to keep his wife happy, so if you are the type of woman who is obsessed with name brand clothes, shoes, makeup products, household goods, etc., you may be perceived as not only a gold digger (I know that feels bad, but it's the truth), but as a woman who is shallow and hard to please and keep happy. No man wants a woman who is hard to please.

Also, men have a fear that if one day something happens and he can no longer afford to support the purchases of these name brand items that his wife will leave. This is one reason that men value humility and supportiveness in a woman so very much.

Does this mean that you should never get anything with a brand name label on it? Of course not, but be balanced, and remember less is best!

3.) Become a thrifty shopper. Couponing, getting things on sale, going to thrift shops and garage sales are small things we can do to be savvier with our money. One thing I have been told this year that sticks out in my mind is that you should never want to pay full price for anything.

4.) Start a clothes swap club or barter club. Clothes swaps are not only a creative and inexpensive way to update your wardrobe, but a time to get together with friends. Pinterest has some really cool ideas for organizing a clothes swap, and any leftover items could easily be donated to a women's shelter!

Not everything is about money my love. Build a network of people whom you can trade time and services with. If you have a special talent, skill, or products that you sell, use those things to leverage for time, services, or products from others within your network. I even know of one woman who bartered her organizing skills with a dentist to get braces for her son!

5.) Start a monthly potluck with your family and close friends. Sharing meals is very cost-effective, not to mention very feminine. If you have neighbors with whom you are close with you can have a neighborhood potluck! What an awesome and cost-effective way to bring people together.

6.) Do your purchases add value and purpose to your life? Establish the needs from the wants. These are the questions that I have started to ask myself whenever I feel the urge to spend money. Do I actually need whatever it is I am wanting to buy? Does it add immense value or purpose to my life, or to the lives of those I love? If I can't answer yes to both questions, I just don't buy it, because I know the purchase is being triggered from an emotional place or it's purely impulsive. Often times we are spending money because we are covering up loneliness, or sadness, or even deep-seated anger, not because we need or even want the thing we are trying to buy. Dig deep before pulling the wallet out of your purse.

7.) Get creative and find fun ways to save money, and learn to make things. Once you really get into it, finding ways to save money can be fun! Try *Groupon* or *Living Social* to find deals on just about anything, but especially beauty services, entertainment, and vacation deals. Go to *YouTube* to find videos on how others are saving money as well. Men you are courting for marriage will look at this and say wow, this woman would really be an asset to the family I'd like to build, and before you know it, you will have several quality men in hot pursuit for your hand in marriage!

8.) Repair your own credit. Having good credit (a score of 700-900) can help you to be an asset to a man that is focused on creating generational wealth. Although I think that the American credit system is a scam in many ways, I understand it to be a necessary evil when it comes to obtaining certain big-name items such as homes, land, and cars. There are many avenues to clean up your credit report, but the easiest way to get started is to simply dispute the items on your credit report. Here's what you do:

First, you need to request your credit reports from all three credit bureaus (Experian, Equifax, and Transunion). You can go directly to the website of each credit bureau or you can go to www.annualcreditreport.com and request a 100% free credit report from all three credit bureaus (by law you have the right to request a free credit report once per year, and any time you have been denied credit).

Secondly, once you have received your credit reports, you need to write a dispute letter to each credit bureau. Each letter needs to have the account information and the reason you are disputing the credit report item. Below is a sample letter:

06/01/2017

Transunion

P.O. Box 2000

Chester, PA 19022

To Whom It May Concern:

I have thoroughly reviewed every line item on my credit report and I need to inform you of the inaccuracies in the report (see list below). I am requesting, under the provisions of the Fair Credit Reporting Act (FCRA), 15 USC section 1681i, that you please investigate these accounts.

Accounts
Reason

(Account Name)   *This collection is not my account*

(Account Number Here)

I understand that failure to investigate these accounts within a 30-day period will result in "non-verification" which requires that the above account/s be immediately removed from my credit report file.

I also understand that the Fair Credit Reporting Act – 15 USC sections 1681i(d) and 1681j- requires that I receive both written notification of the appropriate corrections and updated credit reports at no charge.

Thank you for your time regarding this matter. Have a pleasant day.

Sincerely,

(Sign Your Name)

Your Full Name

Address

Social Security Number

Be sure to list all the accounts you are disputing, and in all honesty you can dispute each and every charge on your credit report. Make sure to send your letters (three separate letters) to each credit bureau with a copy of your driver's license or state issued identification, and a copy of your social security card. You should start receiving decision letters within 30-45 days, and you'll be surprised to see your credit go up significantly within 3 months!

Experian

P.O. Box 9701

Allen, Texas 75013

Equifax

P.O. Box 740241

Atlanta, Georgia 30374

Transunion

P.O. Box 2000

Chester, PA 19022

Chapter Seventeen: Laws of Attraction & Love

What you seek is seeking you – Rumi

I started seriously studying the universal law principles of attraction after being devastatingly crushed by my ex-husband's *final disappearing act*. I struggled to understand why this happened to me when all I did was fast, pray, and try to be good person and a stand-up child of God.

I had heard about the laws of attraction years ago through the movie *The Secret*, and had successfully utilized the principals of the universal laws of attraction to attract many things into my life. So, I needed to make sense of my reality at that time in my life to turn things around, and to have everything I wanted in my life. "Simply put, the Law of Attraction is the ability to attract into our lives whatever we are focusing on. It is believed that regardless of age, nationality, or religious belief, we are a susceptible to the laws which govern the universe – one of which is the Law of Attraction. It is the law of attraction which uses the power of the mind to translate whatever is in our thoughts and materialize it into reality. In basic terms, all thoughts turn into things eventually. If you focus on negative doom and gloom you will remain under that cloud. If you focus on positive thoughts and have goals that you aim to achieve you will find them with mass action.

"This is why the universe is such an infinitely beautiful place, as the Law of Attraction dictates that whatever can be imagined and held in the mind's eye is achievable if you take action on a plan to get to where you want to be." (thelawofattraction.com)

I want you to really understand the amount of influence and power you have in co-creating your manifested reality. I also want you to understand that by being a feminine woman, you have even more manifesting power, because a woman in her feminine essence is very in tune with her feelings. And feelings are needed to activate the laws of attraction.

"Feeling good is the most important thing when it comes to using the Law of Attraction, because how you feel about something is a sign of what you are creating. When you are feeling good, you are in vibrational alignment with the essence of who you really are and with what you want......That is why feeling good needs to be a top priority in your life." (applythelawofattraction.com). This doesn't mean you will never feel bad, or that you should suppress difficult or uncomfortable feelings, but a feminine woman is able to be aware of and feel her full range of emotions so she can quickly adjust, thus changing her point of attraction.

As it relates to love and being a lady in waiting, I believe it is important to think positively about your love life, even if your current reality doesn't match your desire. To increase your ability to attract love into your life, and eventually your husband, I recommend the following tips:

1.) Watch lots of romance movies in which the protagonist gets the guy or there is a happy ending.

2.) Read romance novels

3.) Create space for your husband by cleaning out his side of the closet or dresser. Leave room in your driveway for him to park his car.

4.) Make friends with happily married women.

5.) Sleep on "your" side of the bed.

6.) Speak about your husband and married life.

7.) Start collecting things you will use once married.

8.) Start packing your things to move in with your husband

9.) Start going to the places your ideal guy would go.

10.) Feel him near you.

11.) Believe you can get what you want.

The last thing I'm going to advise you to do is to let it all go. Learn to release it. After all, there are other elements that go into manifesting things like divine timing, and other things we don't have control over. You can only do your part, and in the end, you must trust Benevolent Spirit (God, The Universe) to bring you what you desire.

Chapter Eighteen: It's Ok to Feel Bad

"I found God in myself, and I loved her, I loved her fiercely."

-Ntozake Shange

I know we just talked about the Laws of Attraction, and the importance of feeling good, but the truth is sometimes you will feel bad, and I want you to know it's ok to feel bad. In order for you to work through those awful feelings, and feel better, you need to give yourself permission to have crappy moments. Being able to honor your feelings at all times will allow you to stay in your femininity, and get to your happy place a lot quicker.

The honest truth is sometimes being single sucks. Especially when you reach a particular age, and most people you know are married and have children.

I truly view myself as marriage material and someone's wife, so there are places I go and feel totally out of place because I'm not with my husband. Also, I have made the conscious decision not to become my own husband by doing certain tasks my husband will take care of in the house, so when certain things do need to be done, and there is no man around to take care of things, I can feel the empty space at times. Sometimes that empty space hurts.

The pain of being alone and single is real. People try to down play it, or tell you they wish they were single (and if that's true most of the time, they are married to the wrong person), or they will tell you to simply enjoy your single years, or it will happen when you aren't thinking about it, or some other cliché piece of advice, but the truth is loneliness is real, and something that must be addressed in an honest and frank way.

I will never forget the overwhelming feelings of loneliness when I lived in Miami, many years ago. I had only one friend and after she got married, as many married women do, she gravitated towards her married and engaged friends and I just didn't really see her that often.

The only time the phone rang was for telemarketers, and the only time I had any real socialization was when I attended church, but even that was difficult as many people in the congregation were cliquish and unapproachable. It was just a really tough time for me, and I'm not afraid to say that yes, having a man by my side who was totally in love with me and treating me well, and wanting to marry me would have felt amazingly wonderful.

There are going to be days in waiting where you ask, "Where is this man already?" or going out with your girls, or on trips, or intentional dates, pulling all night Netflix binges, or scrolling your timeline on Facebook, won't feel like enough. Please understand you are normal my love; you are human, dear heart. We were created to be interdependent, desire a life partner, and desire to have babies, so don't beat yourself up when you have your moments.

I also want you to take time to process and feel these difficult feelings of loneliness and sadness, because the quicker you can give yourself permission to feel your feelings, and recognize where you are emotionally, the quicker you can be in the place to raise your vibration and move to a more positive place and stay hopeful that the love of your life will show up.

Chapter Nineteen: Keeping Hope Alive

"I have learned not to worry about love; but to honor its coming with all my heart."

- Alice Walker

There are many things I have done since getting divorced to keep hope alive. I am a hopeless romantic, so I don't think I could ever truly stop believing in love. I want to believe there is a special someone that will grow old with you, and maybe just maybe, if the both of you are lucky enough you will curl up next to each other in bed and drift off into your eternal sleep just like in the movie the Notebook. Here is a list of the top things I do so that I never stop believing in love:

1.) Watch Bollywood Romance movies. Bollywood romance movies are epic. The story lines, colorful outfits, music, and dancing, you will be filled with hope of true love.

2.) Create a romantic playlist for your mp3 or iPod. I listen to music to evoke feelings of love. I've created a special "Calling in The One" playlist. This playlist consists of songs that get me in the mood for love, thinking positively about love and being in a relationship that feels good and supportive, and feeling extra beautiful and feminine!

3.) Surround yourself with those who believe in love and that love is just around the corner. Having other single wives and real wives as friends is encouraging. Surrounding yourself with those who are so passionate about having a happy marriage and being a wife is so important. Their positive attitudes will keep you motivated.

4.) Write love letters to your future husband. I will from time to time write letters of appreciation to my husband letting him know how important he is to the family, and to me, and how I am so blessed to have a man like him in my life. Doing this feels good and helps keep my spirits up.

5.) Wear lots of red, pink, or yellow, these colors are associated with love, hope and happy feelings.

6.) Go to bridal shops and try on wedding dresses. I know this may sound a little crazy, but it's so much fun, and the attention you get from the bridal shop attendants feels so good. This is something you can do with your closest friends and it's also a great visualization tool to really see yourself as a bride.

Final Thoughts

Being a lady in waiting can have its challenges. You will have moments where you will feel lonely, sexually frustrated, and on the verge of losing hope, but it is my desire that this book inspires you to utilize your time as a single wife wisely to become the best woman you can be, not only for yourself, but for your future husband, children, and generations to come.

I leave you with three powerful, real life love stories to help keep your hope alive. The love of your life awaits you. Don't give up!

About the Author

Candice is a Feminine Arts educator, certified life coach, certified relationship coach, and beauty professional from Cleveland, Ohio. Currently residing in sunny Florida, Candice has studied femininity, masculinity, the science of sexual attraction, and male psychology for over 10 years. It has become a passion of hers to help women tap into the power of their feminine essence to attract deeper more intimate relationships with men, foster genuine sisterhood with other women, and have more overall confidence as a woman.

Candice absolutely loves teaching women to enjoy being feminine. She is a traditional woman, with traditional family values, and her overall goal in life is to add value and beauty to the lives of others. She hopes to meet you at one of her workshops soon.

Blissfully Feminine Workshops

You can visit www.blissfullyfeminine.com to contact Candice regarding her Intentional Dating program, a unique course designed for marriage-minded women who want to date with purpose. You can also check out her other workshops, as well as activities that she hosts year-round.

Our Love Story: Aneesah & Asad

Aneesah and her husband Asad met mid-summer of 2012 and married a short 2 months later in September of 2012. Aneesah and Asad both being devout orthodox Muslims met and fell in love the traditional Islamic way.

Asad had been looking for a good wife and made inquiries about Aneesah. Hearing that she was in fact single, he approached her brother to see if she was open to the possibility of getting to know him for the purpose of getting married.

When Aneesah first heard that he was interested I her, she immediately became terrified. It had been five years since she had gotten divorced from her daughter's father, who was very abusive. She had told herself the next time she got married, that she would initiate the entire process. She had seen Asad around the community, but didn't know much about him. Her brother convinced her to meet him by reminding her that it was just an introduction and there was no pressure.

Shortly after being introduced the Islamic Holy Month of Ramadan began. The two both decided to wait until after Ramadan to start formally communicating. She would see him during that time and never once did he stop and casually talk to her (something that more conservative Muslims find inappropriate among unmarried Muslims). It was very important to Aneesah that he showed the utmost respect and adherence to her conservative Islamic values.

Once they did start communicating they wasted no time in asking each other the important questions to see if they were truly compatible for each other and could build a life together. In this discovery process, Aneesah realized that she had pre-judged Asad, and soon found herself falling in love with him.

Once they were married, they found that deciding how to discipline the children, (they both had children from previous marriages) was an issue. After being married for five years, and lots of communication, they have finally come to a common understanding as to the best way to discipline the children.

The best relationship advice Aneesah has ever gotten is to always make time for your spouse. "Life can get pretty hectic and from the beginning, we both had busy schedules". After speaking to a friend about how busy they were, a suggestion for "date night" was made. Incorporating a regular date night really made a big difference in their marriage.

The one thing Aneesah wishes she had known prior to marriage is the importance of asking the important questions. Being that her marriage to Asad was her second time around, she felt more prepared. She had come across an article with 100 questions to ask your potential spouse, and she referred to those questions while getting to know Asad, she even spoke to his ex-wife to get her side of why their marriage didn't work out. Aneesah, being a survivor of domestic violence (from her first marriage), also wishes she knew about the red flags of domestic violence. She felt good knowing that Asad showed no signs of being an abusive person.

The one thing Aneesah wants everyone reading this book to know is that when someone loves you, they show it rather than just give you lip service. You may not understand why your spouse may like things a certain way, but showing that you are sensitive to the wants and needs of your partner is love.

Our Love Story: Nisha & Khalil

Nisha was introduced to her husband through her husband's cousin, who was her friend from High School. Khalil's sincerity towards people and his ability to hold an intelligent conversation is what drew Nisha to Khalil.

Nisha knew that Khalil was the one for her when they both decided to change their lifestyle. They were both wanting to live a slower pace of life, and he was willing to support Nisha's desire to do that. They both agreed to put the toxicity behind them and start a brand-new life together.

What brought them closer together as a couple was going through infertility struggles. Nisha and Khalil suffered three pregnancy losses and it was emotionally devastating. With the both the emotional and financial support of their families, they went through fertility treatment and had a baby boy. The experience of the losses and the joy of finally having a child of their own solidified their marriage.

The one thing that Nisha wishes she understood prior to getting married is the importance of saving her virginity for her husband. When you really love someone, you learn the true meaning of intimacy, and how priceless your virginity is as a woman.

The one thing Nisha wants the women who read this book to know is that love is not JUST about physical attraction. Love is about being able to depend on one another and accept one another when times are bad. The best piece of relationship advice she has ever gotten is to not sweat the small stuff in relationships, and pick your battles. If a minor thing like your husband not picking up his wet towels, bothers you, and your spouse won't fix it, then just do it yourself and move on. Sometimes you must weigh all that your husband does right, against the minor things he doesn't do so that the relationship stays positive.

Our Love Story: Stefan & Carissa

Stefan and Carissa met in 2011. He was browsing through Facebook and saw her picture. He thought she was gorgeous, probably one of the prettiest women he had ever seen in his life. He noticed that they had mutual interests and mutual friends so he clicked the "request friend" button, and the rest is history as they say.

After she accepted his request she later learned that he owned an online radio station. A couple of weeks later he attended a "game night" event, specifically because he knew she would be there and he wanted to see her. He really wanted to meet her in person, and that's exactly what he did. He showed up to the event, met her, and immediately left because he had no interest in hanging out or getting to know anyone else there.

After being "Facebook Friends" for years and only seeing each other twice in real life, they started conversing more and more in early January when Carissa called Stefan wanting help with her website. By that March, he knew he wanted her to be his. In May, they made their courtship official with him asking her father for the opportunity to date her.

What made Carissa stand out from any other woman he had met previously was that she had a joy for life that was evidenced in every word she spoke and every move she made. He could tell this was a woman devoted to embracing life no matter what life threw at her. She was amazingly outgoing and truly interested in getting to know the people she interacted with. He could tell there were no ulterior motives, or hidden agendas. She cared about people and was interested in receiving the knowledge, wisdom, and experience life had to offer.

, it didn't take long for him to figure out she was going to be his. After they got to know each other a little better, he gave her an opportunity he had never extended to anyone, and that was to really get to know him in a vulnerable and intimate way. They participated in a vulnerability challenge, in which she could ask him any 10 questions she wanted and he was required to tell the truth, the whole truth, and nothing but the truth. Over the course of about a month she asked question after question, and he never hesitated to give her the full truth. No matter how, self-conscious he may have been about the thing she was asking, no matter how embarrassing the response came across, no matter how much he felt like keeping on his mask, he told her the truth. He was comfortable doing it and wasn't afraid to let her in.

It was then he knew that there was something special about this woman. She was able to let his guard down without being abrasive, whiny, or manipulative. It was at this point he decided that he was

going to marry this woman, and he knew he couldn't waste any time making it happen. She would later say she could tell that he wasn't playing around and that "she had to prepare herself for a proposal she knew would be coming". This was even before they made their relationship official and he had spoken to her father about marrying her.

What has made their relationship stronger is the fact that they live in two different cities across the state from each other. Although the distance isn't far enough away to be monumental, it's far enough not to be incidental. The distance has kept them intentional about their relationship. It's made them stay aware of each other's hearts and helped them stay alert to each other's feelings. They regularly check up on each other and make sure the other person feels heard, attended to and loved.

The best relationship advice that Stefan has been given is that marriage illuminates the sin in our lives. For him, this is the greatest truth he has ever known. "Marriage and the relationship leading up to it, will show you the areas you've been selfish, trigger the hidden hurts and unforgiveness you've buried. It is a mirror that shows you everything you've tried to hide, and if you use it correctly, it can help you become the person you've always known you were or dreamed you could be." Stefan says.

The one thing he wishes he knew prior to getting engaged is to embrace the weight of responsibility that comes with loving a woman correctly. "I wish someone had given me insight on the daily choices I would have to make and why it was important to make them. I wish someone had told me how the smile of the woman you were made to protect can reach a depth in your heart you never knew existed."

What Stefan wants all the wonderful women who read this book to know is that when a man has chosen you, you will NEVER have to question his love. Love is a choice not a feeling. So many people will agree to this and then want to make decisions about their love

based on feelings. His choice can outlast a million hurricanes and a trillion earthquakes. He wants you to know that YOU are more than a wife to him, you are the foundation for his purpose. "I'm not saying his life will or should revolve around you, but I am saying... He works hard to see you happy." "He sacrifices so that you may enjoy the youth of your children. He takes on burdens so you won't worry. He heaps responsibilities on his shoulders so that you will smile at him in such a way that no other woman's smile will matter. He chooses these things every day because he loves you. Don't let your temporary feelings take that away."

Made in the USA
Lexington, KY
28 July 2017